IMAGES OF ENGLAND

AROUND
DERBY

IMAGES OF ENGLAND

AROUND DERBY

ALAN CHAMPION
AND MARK EDWORTHY

Frontispiece: The Shot Tower in the Morledge seen here shortly before its demolition in 1932.

First published in 1994 by Tempus Publishing Limited
New Edition 2003

Reprinted in 2011 by
The History Press
The Mill, Brimscombe Port,
Stroud, Gloucestershire, GL5 2QG
www.thehistorypress.co.uk

© Alan Champion and Mark Edworthy, 2011

The right of Alan Champion and Mark Edworthy to be identified as the
Author of this work has been asserted in accordance with the Copyrights,
Designs and Patents Act 1988.

All rights reserved. No part of this book may be reprinted or reproduced or
utilised in any form or by any electronic, mechanical or other means, now
known or hereafter invented, including photocopying and recording, or in
any information storage or retrieval system, without the permission in writing
from the Publishers.

British Library Cataloguing in Publication Data.
A catalogue record for this book is available from the British Library.

ISBN 978 0 7524 3014 0

Typesetting and origination by Tempus Publishing Limited
Printed and bound in Great Britain

Contents

The fire brigade of Ley's Foundry in Colombo Street who won the all England Challenge Bowl Championship in 1939.

Introduction

The essence of this book is nostalgia. We are both Derby men, with a long- standing interest in the town. Although now a city, people of our generation and the generation before still refer to Derby as a "town", a habit which we fear will be hard to break.

We have lived through one of the greatest periods of change in Derby's history. Many of the streets we remember from thirty years ago have gone. Many buildings have sadly disappeared, to be replaced by characterless shops and offices.

In compiling this book we have tapped our own collections of picture postcards and photographs, together with those of friends and family. Many of the pictures have never been published before and combine familiar scenes, which thankfully remain much the same a century later, with the more unusual views. We have included some personalities and characters whom some readers may remember with a smile. We have cast our net a little wider than the boundaries of the town and have included suburbs and villages that can be reached by a good walk or short ride.

The book spans a period of over one hundred years, roughly the period of the picture postcard. We rely heavily on our local photographers. In this we are lucky. Derby had three superb exponents of the art, all of who had an eye for an interesting and imaginative photograph. Richard Keene was responsible for most of the earlier views of Derby. F.W. Scarratt's postcards cover the reigns of Edward VII and George V, while W.W. Winter still operates today. In addition, many photographs are found which give no clue to the photographer's identity, and we gratefully acknowledge the work of these unsung recorders of Derby's history.

We hope that this glimpse of Derby over the last five generations will provide an interesting and possibly thought-provoking tour through Derby's photographic past.

Alan Champion and Mark Edworthy

All Saints Church, now the Cathedral, viewed from Iron Gate in 1907.

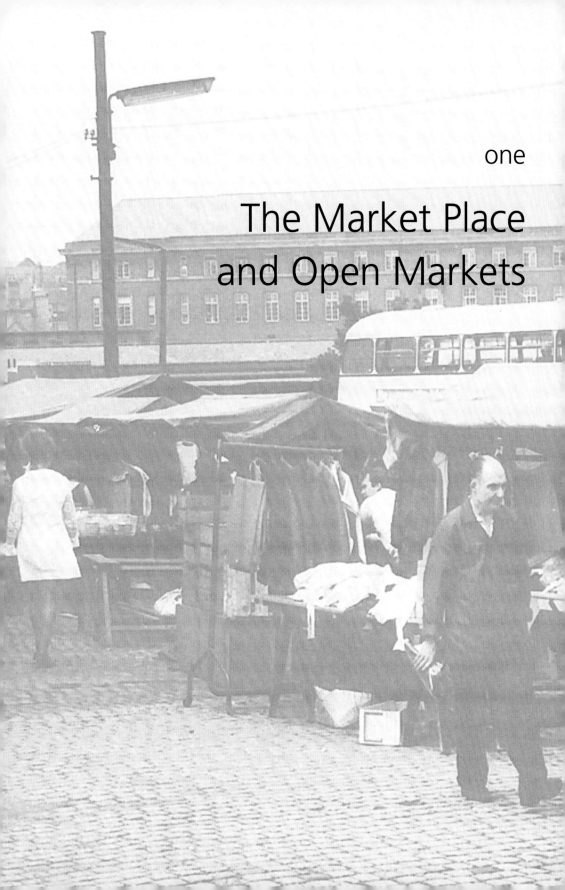

one

The Market Place
and Open Markets

Above: The Market Place
c. 1920 on Market day.

Left: A view of Rotten Row
and Iron Gate looking north.
The Piazzas and the eastern
end of Rotten Row which
were demolished in 1869-70
are on the right. The original
entrance to Iron Gate can also
be seen.

Opposite above: Rotten Row,
with the entrance to Sadler
Gate on the left.

Opposite below: A view of Iron
Gate looking north before the
widening. The width of the
street at this end was, until
the year 1866, under 16 feet.
Accidents were a frequent
occurrence.

An impressive group in the Market Place. The Mayor, his legal officers, and a member of the Derbyshire Yeomanry *c.* 1920.

This shows the north end of the old Piazzas, and the eastern side of the Rotten Row, taken from the entrance to Irongate after it had been widened. The Corn Market can be seen in the distance.

Iron Gate in the 1920s.

The Corn Market *c.* 1930.

South side of the Market Square (sic) shortly after the demolition of the old Piazzas in 1871. This is believed to be the only surviving photograph to show the full frontage of the old Royal Oak Inn at this time.

Market Place *c.* 1910.

The Prince of Wales, later to be King Edward the Eighth, inspecting Derby veterans in the Market Place c. 1930.

The Market Place on a damp day in the early 1960s.

Cockpit Hill *c.* 1955.

Cockpit Hill market in the 1950s. One of the best free shows in town, with "Mad Harry's" stall guaranteed to draw a crowd.

The Morledge *c.* 1906 with the shot tower in the background.

The market area in the 1920s.

The old established Hay and Corn Stores at the turn of the century. Its exact location is now something of a mystery, but it was probably near Cockpit Hill.

The Easter Fair in 1913 with Harry Hall's gallopers on the right.

Inside the Market Hall *c.* 1920. This picture was taken by F.W. Scarratt, and shows his own shop on the far end of the balcony. The Market Hall was built by Tho rburn in 1864, at a cost of £29,000. The roof is a single span, supported by cast-iron ribs, and measures an impressive 220 feet by 112 feet.

Looking down on the bus station during its construction. It was built by Gee, Walker, and Slater, in art-deco style and was opened in 1933.

The Morledge *c.* 1960.

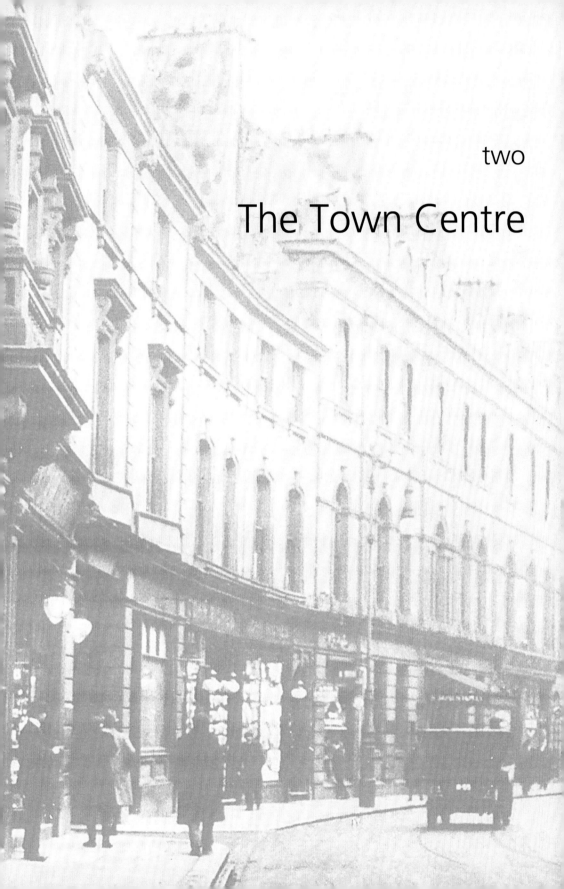

two

The Town Centre

Above: St Peter's Street, *c.* 1925.

Right: East Street in the days when one could drive along it, with a delivery van outside the Midland Drapery.

Opposite above: A fine animated view of St Peter's Street *c.* 1930.

Opposite below: The Midland Drapery, one of Derby's most popular department stores on the corner of St Peter's Street and East Street.

St Peter's Street looking towards the Corn Market *c.* 1906.

Victoria Street *c.* 1909.

A bustling scene in St. Peter's Street *c*. 1930.

St James's Street in the early part of the century after widening.

Above: Victoria Street *c.* 1930.

Left: Plenty of people wanting to get in the picture of St James's Lane at the Corn Market end. The order for the widening of this lane was obtained in 1866. It was renamed St James's Street, and housed the new post office and St James's Hotel, then the largest in Derby.

Looking along the Strand towards Cheapside. The buildings have now disappeared, and have been replaced with the extension to the museum and art gallery.

Opposite view of the same corner.

London Road looking towards the Spot with a tram in front of the Congregational Church, later to become the Coliseum cinema.

One of Derby's many amateur football teams in a *Derby Evening Telegraph* photo of the 1930s.

Friar Gate before Ford Street (on the right) was widened.

Friar Gate in the 1950s.

A nice advert for Edgar Horne and Co. in the Strand. Mr Kennerly Rumford was an opera singer who married the far more famous Miss, later to be Dame, Clara Butt.

Above: Friar Gate 1926. This scene has remained remarkably unchanged. Simpson's the printers looked the same outside (and in!) until its recent closure. The Derby Gas, Light, and Coke Company building is on the right.

Right: This off-licence stood in Friar Gate and was later to become Tomlinson's, the ironmonger.

Above: Opened by the Duchess of Rutland in 1894, the Deaf and Dumb Institute in Friar Gate was the lifetimes work of W.R. Roe, its founder and headmaster. He devoted his life to the education of the deaf, and lectured on the subject all over the world. The opening ceremony was performed with the aid of some electrical wizardry devised by the town's lighting engineer, the main door being opened by remote control when a switch was operated.

Above: The Spot in the early years of the twentieth century.

Opposite below: Friar Gate, looking towards town, *c.* 1910.

Royal Infirmary *c.* 1908.

Cheapside *c.* 1905.

A large crowd in the Corn Market for the visit of Queen Victoria in 1891. The Queen came to lay the foundation stone of the Derbyshire Royal Infirmary. Later in the day, at an impromptu ceremony, she knighted the Mayor Alfred Haslam at the Railway Station.

A man wheels a cart along the tram-lines of London Road *c.* 1910.

Station Street, *c.* 1910, now called Midland Road.

A busy scene in Midland Road. The small amount of traffic at this time, can be assumed from the number of people sauntering down the middle of the road.

The opening of the Margaret Dondney Home, named after the matron. She is seen here in the centre of the picture in the white hat. She is holding a box containing a gold key which was presented to her to unlock the door. The nursing home was situated off London Road, opposite the Derbyshire Royal Infirmary.

Above: Derby from the long bridge *c.* 1905.

Left: St Alkmund's Church Spire, two hundred feet tall, used to dominate the skyline, but was demolished to make way for the inner ring road.

Opposite: The annual tradition of well-dressing is seen all over Derbyshire. Here, St Alkmund's well in Well Street is seen in 1924. This well was first dressed in 1857, and was accompanied by a Sunday-school procession. Happily this well survives, along with the tradition of well-dressing.

Above: The Grand Theatre, Babington Lane in 1912. The theatre was opened 25 March 1886 and gutted by fire six weeks later. It was rebuilt, and reopened six months afterwards.

Left: The Jacobean House in the Wardwick on the right was a far more impressive building before Beckett Street was driven through. This picture is a perfect snap-shot of Edwardian Derby with the delivery carts, road sweeper, and boys in their high-collared shirts and plus-twos.

Nottingham Road bridge in 1935. The road was lowered to allow trams and trolleybuses to pass under the railway. Unfortunately the dip in the road used to flood, but some vehicles were still able to pass under the bridge on the wide raised pavement to the left of the road in this picture.

Cemetery Hill, Nottingham Road, taken from a postcard used in August 1927.

Looking towards Albert Street and the Market.

The Cornmarket. On 22 May 1932 the culvert of Markeaton brook overflowed flooding much of the town centre. In only thirty-six hours, 3.25 inches of rain had fallen with the devastating results that can be seen in these pictures.

Sadler Gate.

Derby's First World War V.C., Private Jacob Rivers. He was awarded the V.C. posthumously for two acts of gallantry on the same day. At Neuve Chappelle on 12 March 1915, he twice attacked large groups of the enemy single handed, throwing bombs on them. He was killed during the second attack, and his body was never recovered.

three

Sport, Leisure, and a Royal Visit

The hundred acres of Markeaton Park have been a popular place to relax for many years. The former owner of the park, Mrs Mundy, would allow school parties to visit as a special treat. She left the hall and park to the Corporation of Derby who unfortunately allowed the hall to fall into disrepair and it was demolished in 1964. All that remains of the building is the orangery.

The aviary in the arboretum *c.* 1912.

In the 1920s the wild boar must have been worn smooth by the number of children who sat astride it. This is quite a rare picture without a boy sitting proudly on its back.

Arboretum entrance in 1911.

The Arboretum was given to the town by Joseph Strutt. Opened in 1840, it was the first public park in England.

Normanton recreation ground. The pavilion was opened by the Duke of Devonshire on 4 September 1904. The buildings to the left have been replaced with totally inappropriate modern constructions.

Thomas Stanley Worthington, known universally as Stan. The Derbyshire all-rounder was one of the few players from the County to be capped by England. He toured Australia in 1929-30, and was capped again in 1936, the year of Derbyshire's one and only championship victory. He scored a century at the Oval, sharing in a record partnership with Wally Hammond.

A candid shot at Derby Regatta in 1912. The photographer has managed to catch most of his subjects with their backs to the camera.

Opposite above: Darley Park looking towards the Hall. This eighteenth-century house was left to the town in 1925, and used as a school for some years. Like many local halls, it has now been demolished.

Opposite below: Band of Hope demonstration in Derwent Park, 1904. They were one of many temperance groups in Derby.

DARLEY ABBEY PARK, DERBY   G. 2582

BAND OF HOPE DEMONSTRATION
DERWENT PARK   25·6·04

P. Wyld.   F. H. Wyld.   R. Wyld.   L. A. Wyld
            ·Champion·

The Wyld brothers were well known in the 1920s and 1930s, drawing large crowds when they raced at the Municipal cycle track. The brothers were selected to compete in the 1928 Olympics.

The Midland station decorated ready for King Edward VII's visit in 1906. Everyone is in their Sunday best. The chauffeur-driven car is not waiting for the King, he travelled by carriage.

Looking along Midland Road towards the station, as the crowds begin to gather for the King's visit in 1906.

King Edward VII passes the Spot on his way to open the Royal Show.

It always seemed to rain for important events. The umbrellas are out as the people wait to catch a glimpse of King Edward outside Mason's Paints in Derwent Street.

The farmer's club at the Royal Show.

The Derby Royal Field Artillery football team in 1915.

The entrance of the Royal Show Ground in 1906. The show was held in a different town each year, which involved dismantling, and transporting all the buildings to the new venue.

Derby County in Cup-winning year. This is the victorious semi-final team. The 1946 final was watched by the King and Princess Elizabeth, who was much amused by the famous incident of the bursting ball.

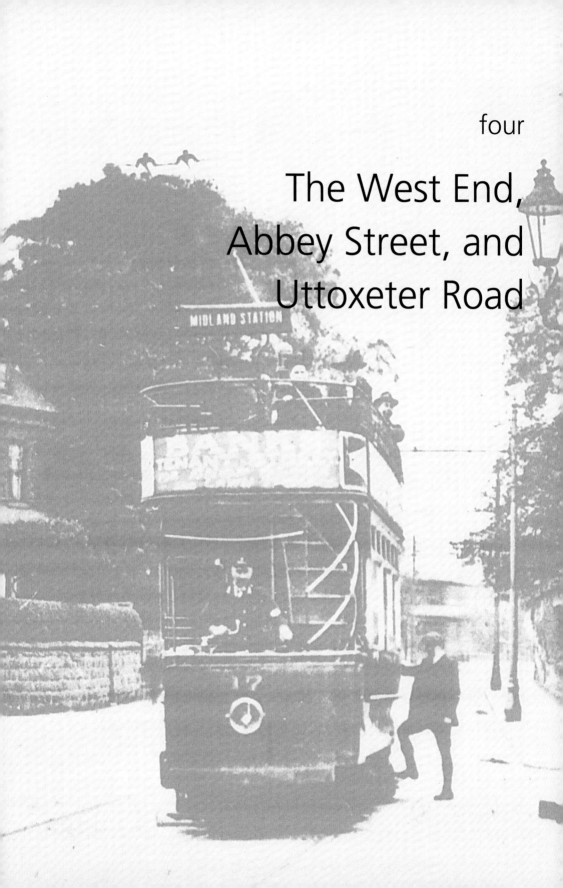

four

The West End, Abbey Street, and Uttoxeter Road

Five lamps on the corner of Kedleston Road and Duffield Road *c.* 1910.

Duffield Road still retains its charm with the raised pavement and ironwork more than one hundred years after this photograph was taken.

Bill Morley whose cycle and radio shop was in Brook Street. A well known character in the west end, and on Derby's open market.

Edith Morley, wife of Bill, who lived in Whitecross Street.

Hospital day in the 1920s. McCann's were based in Monk Street, but the exact location of the photograph is unknown.

St Anne's Church Procession of Witness in 1927. St Anne's Church was in Whitecross Street.

Miss Campbell's keep-fit class of 1927 preparing to demonstrate Indian-club swinging.

Kedleston Road looking from Cedar Street. The vinegar factory on the right became the "Maltings" nursing home.

Empire Day celebrations at Kedleston Road School, 23 May 1913.

Kedleston Road, near Bromley Street, in 1910.

Above: Wathall's of Macklin Street. The building is still recognisable, although the frontage has been much altered.

Right: Derby Municipal Secondary School was in Abbey Street. The school was founded in 1874, and closed one hundred years later.

WITH KINDEST REGARDS
AND BEST WISHES
from all the
MASTERS AND BOYS
to all the
"OLD BOYS"
Who are serving their Country on
Sea or Land.

" Then the cloud-rift broadens,
spanning earth that's under,
Wide our world displays its worth,
man's strife and strife's success."

Christmas, 1918.

A pub outing from the Curzon Arms at the corner of Monk Street and Abbey Street. The pub was closed in 1929, and then demolished.

North Parade looking from River Street.

Lynton Street near Uttoxeter New Road has changed little since 1910. The houses remain, but the chapel on the left has disappeared, to be replaced by a block of flats.

SOLE MAKER OF
Real Derby Butterscotcl

To quote from an early guide to Derby, "Visitors to Derby who are interested in the manufacture of high-class sweetmeats, should pay a visit to J.E. Chattell Crown Works, Abbey Street. Absolute cleanliness and purity of materials used have contributed to the success of this up to date firm. The famous Derby Butterscotch is made here."

The chapel in Dean Street, off Stockbrook Street, *c.* 1910.

Bemrose School pictured shortly after its completion in 1930. The photographer must have been perilously close to the cricket square, desecration of which was almost a hanging offence!

This postcard of Burton Road was mailed in October 1918. From a postcard collector's point of view, it is almost the perfect card, containing a close view of a tram with lots of animation provided by the pedestrians.

Whitaker Road *c.* 1912.

five

The Suburbs

St Thomas's Road *c.* 1910 with a group of children in warm clothing, squinting into a low sun.

The end of Stenson Road with the Cavendish Hotel on the right, which gave its name to this area of Derby.

Stenson Road, Derby.

Above: Stenson Road at the Cavendish end, with an imposing Derby Co-op store on the right. Sadly, this delightful frontage has become a victim of 'modernisation'.

Left: Mr Boyes and his butcher's boy outside their shop on Stenson Road.

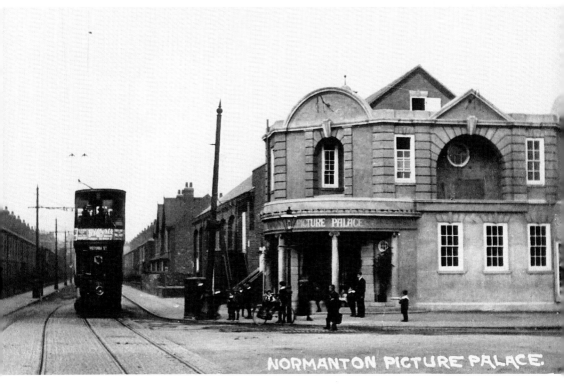

Normanton Picture Palace.

St. James' Church Oliver Institute on Dairy House Road.

Burton Road looking from Abbey Street. The tall chimney in the distance was called Mount Carmel Tower, which was part of Mason's Paints factory. The building was designed in an elaborate Moorish style by Edwin Thompson in 1869.

Empress Road *c.* 1912.

Burton Road, looking up the hill from Abbey Street *c.* 1920.

This postcard is captioned "Littleover Hill". It is of course now known as Burton Road, just below Whitaker Road.

An election meeting captured by the photographer W.W. Winter. Sir Herbert Raphael was a London banker, who came to Derby to stand for the safe seat of Derby South. While in Derby he lived in Allestree Hall, and was made a Lord in 1911.

The vicarage was demolished in 1963 and bungalows built on the site, the new avenue being named Old Vicarage Close.

Church Street Littleover in 1926.

The authors' extensive research into the Half Moon Inn has revealed it to be a mainly Victorian building, although an inn has occupied this site for over 400 years.

St Peter's second eleven, Littleover, in the 1920s.

The old post office in Littleover in 1907.

Burton Road, Littleover, looking from Heath Avenue in about 1930. Freestone's general store on the left is now an opticians, but the chemist's shop remains.

Littleover Hollow, Derby.

F.W. Scarratt, the photographer, liked to ensure an interesting view. He usually took members of his family along to appear in the picture. Here, his brothers are seen in the centre, while Scarratt's own motorcycle is carefully parked on the left.

The recently-demolished County Asylum, Mickleover.

The Hollow, Mickleover, *c.* 1906, is still recognisable today, although the cottages have been altered.

Mickleover school, Uttoxeter Road, first built in 1881 and enlarged in 1905. Infants were first admitted in 1916, which is about the date of this photograph. It closed as a school in 1957, and is now a community centre.

Mickleover Wesleyan Chapel is on Station Road. The laying of the foundation stone is seen here in 1914. It became Mickleover Methodist Church in 1932, and was further extended in 1956 and 1968.

Mackworth Castle dates from the fifteenth century, and was a fortified manor house of the Mackworth family. Local folklore says that the castle was attacked by Cromwell's army during the Civil War and a local prominence nearby is called 'Canon Hill'.

New Chester Street *c.* 1910. The Garden City Inn is still on the corner, but the rest of the street has now disappeared.

Chapel Street Kilburn *c.* 1910. Note the photographer's motor cycle parked on the left of the picture.

Breadsall Church after the fire, 5 June 1914. Revd J.A. Whitaker, the parish priest, was convinced it was the work of the suffragettes, or "Mad Women" as he called them. A hat-pin was found near the window through which the arsonist made his or her entrance. The window was small, which also pointed to a young woman, rather than a man, as the perpetrator, but nothing was proved. The interior of the 900-year-old church was damaged beyond repair.

A group enjoying a pint after a game of cricket. The brewer is Zachary Smith of Shardlow.

An old forge near Derby but the exact location is unknown.

Alice Grace was born in 1867. When her mother died she was unable to pay the rent on the family cottage. She made her home in a bacon box on Whitaker Lane, Little Eaton. The villagers would throw her coins, one of which she always kept in her shoe to prevent a charge of vagrancy. Eventually she was persuaded to move to the Shardlow Institution, where she died in 1927.

Alvaston Church *c.* 1910.

Alvaston Lake in the 1920s.

The Welcome, Brighton Road, Alvaston. It opened as a temperance hotel, but closed in the early 1950s.

Looking down on the High Street from Chellaston Church Tower, c. 1930.

The Lodge to Spondon Hall *c.* 1908. The Hall itself was demolished in the mid 1950s and houses built on the site. The drive to the hall is now called Willowcroft Road.

The Smithy, Spondon *c.* 1908.

six

Shops,
Public Houses
and Industry

Mason's shop *c.* 1906.

QUALITY IS THE TEST OF CHEAPNESS.

MASON & SON,

31 Sadler Gate, DERBY,

Supply everything to make the "HOUSE-BEAUTIFUL."

Mayresco, absolutely the Best Washable Distemper.

Temerare, a cheap Colour Wash. Very satisfactory.

Wall Paper, Large Variety. latest designs.

Paint, mixed from genuine English White Lead. Any tint matched.

Enamel, for all purposes by the Leading Makers.

Stained Varnishes, for Furniture, Floors, etc. Any Colour.

French Polish, made on the Premises to Customer's Requirements.

Ishineall, Gold Enamel for Picture Frames, etc. **Next Best to 22-carat Gold Leaf.**

Stained Glass (Imitation), Variety of Design suitable for any window, etc.

W. & N. Artists' Materials kept in stock.

Turpentine
Linseed Oil } Best procurable.
Meth. Spirit

Gen. Aluminium Enamel.

Brushes of every description for Painting and Decorating.

SPECIAL TERMS TO DECORATORS AND PROPERTY OWNERS.

Henry Ault, poultry salesman, seen outside his shop on the corner of London Road and Harrow Street in 1903.

The Exchange Dining Rooms on the corner of what is now Osnabruck Square. The building was recently knocked down, and a Laura Ashley shop built in its place.

The Grange Hotel, Normanton. Opened as a public house in 1932 by the Derby brewery Offilers.

This picture by W.W. Winter shows a group of First World War volunteers. Someone has pencilled "Normanton Barracks" on the back of the photograph, but the buildings in the background look more like a factory.

The Lord Raglan, in Clover Street, named after the Crimean war hero. Rather a grand title for such a small pub.

No chance of missing the name on famous this store in Victoria Street.

RANBY'S,

THE PEOPLE'S

General and Fancy Drapery Warehouse,

17, 18, 19, 20, 21, 22, 23, 24,

VICTORIA ST., DERBY.

Wires—"RANBY'S, DERBY."   Telephone 298.

The Wagon and Horses by the tram terminus on Ashbourne Road. When this photograph was taken in 1910, the landlord (seen here) was E. Morley.

Above: Liptons shop in St Peter's Street, or the Corn Market.

Left: The Carlton Hotel on London Road is an attractive Georgian building near the junction with Midland Road.

The Lifeboat in Wilson Street, famous as Derby's smallest public house. The bar was simply the converted front room of a small terraced cottage. Sadly demolished in the 1980s.

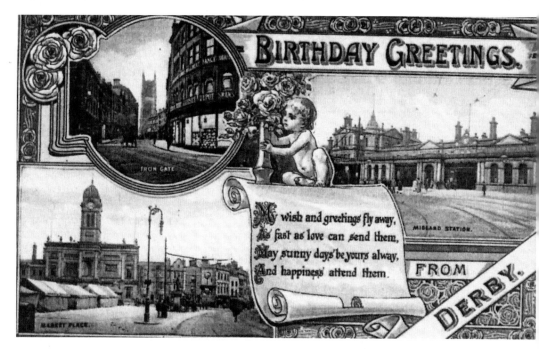

An Edwardian Greetings Card with three views of Derby.

Based at the Station Hotel, Midland Road, the Leigh family cricket eleven in 1910.

The Old Dolphin in Queen Street. This claims to be the oldest public house in Derby dating from 1530.

The opening of a Co-op store in about 1930. This was the boom-time for the Co-op, with dozens of shops all over Derby and its suburbs.

Above: Abbey Street looking towards the Pelican Inn on the corner of Stockbrook Street. The pub was demolished in 1979.

Right: The grocer's shop at the corner of Harrison Street with an impressive display of enamel advertising signs.

Pumping Station, Derby Corporation Waterworks.

Opposite: Richard Bell, MP for Derby City. He was born in Merthyr in 1859, and worked for the Great Western Railway. His association with the Amalgamated Society of Railway Servants resulted in his nomination to become MP for Derby. He was known as the Railwayman's MP.

Canoes and rowing boats on the Derwent outside the Bridge Inn, Mansfield Road.

Several onlookers watch from the bridge as an oarsman passes beneath them.

seven

Transport

Horse omnibus operated by Derby Tramways Company, photographed at Alvaston. Another advertisement for Edgar Horne appears on the side.

Above: The Ashbourne Road horse tram service survived longer than any of the other horse tram routes. When this beautifully-posed photograph was taken in 1907, electric trams had been running in other parts of Derby for nearly three years.

Opposite below: This photograph was actually taken in 1949! Horse omnibus No. 2 again takes to the streets for the fiftieth anniversary of Derby Corporation Omnibus Department. The setting is Ascot Drive trolleybus depot.

Above: With a load of less than happy passengers, this Derby-registered motor car sets out on another expedition.

Opposite above: Electric Car No. 12 (in original form) and crew pose for a photograph at Abingdon Street Tram Depot *c.* 1904.

Opposite below: Tram Terminus Alvaston.

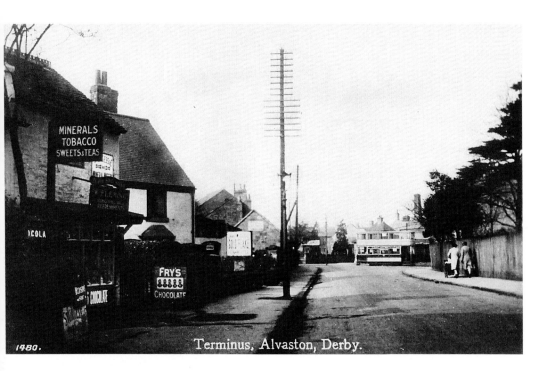

Terminus, Alvaston, Derby.

Above: This photograph of car No. 78 in final form is dated 2 July 1934, the last day of electric tramcar operation in Derby.

Opposite above: A charabanc outing from the Park Tavern in Park Street in the 1920s.

Opposite below: Victoria Street in the early 1920s with the rear end of a Derby Corporation battery-electric bus just visible. This bus was withdrawn from service in 1924, some eight years before the introduction to Derby of overhead-powered trolleybuses.

The erecting shop of Derby's Locomotive Works in LMS days. The LMS railway owned over 7,000 locomotives, many of which were built here.

The First World War roll of honour in No. 9 shop of the Derby Locomotive Works.

Trolleybus No. 100, a Dodson-bodied Sunbeam, undergoes its tilt test before delivery to Derby in 1932. Quite a reassuring demonstration!

North Stafford 0-6-2T No. 1 leaving Derby.

A group of local motor-cyclists seen during a particularly hard winter.

During the Second World War, Derby Corporation was desperately short of serviceable buses. A batch of six second-hand single-deck trolleybuses were purchased from Hastings. It is said that these vehicles were in poor condition and had been abandoned in a field prior to sale to Derby. Only four of the six ever ran in service here, and they were replaced within three years. However, No. 165, photographed in Albert Street in 1942, looks superficially tidy after repainting.

The crew returns to motorbus No. 78 parked in Tenant Street. The advantages of opening windscreens in hot summers are plain to see.

Buses are no longer allowed in Derby's Market Place, the layout of which provided ample room for well-spaced bus stands. Here, motorbus No. 20 awaits its passengers (and crew) by the Tenant Street corner.

A fully-laden Sunbeam trolleybus of 1949 vintage heads into town from the Midland Station. This batch of Brush-bodied trolleybuses were fitted with traction batteries and in an emergency could run slowly to the nearest live section of overhead. The batteries were also used on occasions for manœuvring at the depot.

Motor Bus No.36 crosses Sinfin Lane Bridge before it was widened.

A Derby Airways DC3 "Dakota" which operated from Burnaston Airport, now the Toyota car factory. The airport was opened 17 June 1939.

A post-war view of trolleybus No 139. In spite of its apparent size, this Brush-bodied Guy six-wheeler only seated fifty-six passengers.

Delivered new in 1948, these non-utility vehicles were the first 8' wide buses used by Derby Corporation. All previous buses being of only 7'6" width.

Trolleybus 215 photographed at the end of June 1967, some ten weeks before the Derby trolleybus system closed. The driver saw the camera and obligingly stopped the bus and applied the handbrake while the author took this photograph. The author, in turn, liked the photograph so much he bought the trolleybus. It still runs at trolleybus rallies today.

Acknowledgements

Our special thanks go to Maxwell Craven, and Alan Doig. Thanks also to:

Mick Allseybrook, Mark Bown, Mary Buckler, Clive Champion, Edna Champion, *Derby Evening Telegraph*, Derby Local Studies Library, Rod Jewell, Mic Newbold, Don Storer, Mick White.